NATIONAL GEOGRAPHIC

Jupiter
The Moon King

PIONEER EDITION

By Beth Geiger and Ray Villard

CONTENTS

Jupiter
The Moon King

Jupiter is an amazing planet. Everything about it is big. It is the largest planet in our solar system. Huge storms rage on its surface. Yet Jupiter may be best known for its many moons.

Jupiter looms above Ganymede.

Galileo

Planet Jupiter

Jupiter is the fifth planet from the sun. It is quite different from Earth. The planet is cooler than Earth. It is much larger too. Nearly 1,400 Earths could fit inside this giant! Jupiter is not solid like Earth. It is made mostly of gases.

Many Moons

Jupiter is different in another way too. Earth has just one **moon.** Jupiter has at least 63! There may be even more. A moon is a natural object that circles a planet.

Most of Jupiter's moons are small. But four are very large. A scientist named Galileo (gah lih LAY oh) spotted them 400 years ago. Today, they are called the Galilean moons. Let's take a closer look at them.

Io

Io is nearer to Jupiter than the other Galilean moons. It is also hotter. Many volcanoes erupt on Io. They make it look like a pizza.

Europa

A thick layer of ice covers Europa. The ice is ten miles thick. Under it lies a hidden ocean. This may be 50 miles deep.

Ganymede

Ganymede is Jupiter's largest moon. It is nearly 3,300 miles across. That makes it the largest moon in our solar system.

Callisto

Callisto looks like it has freckles. Why? Many **meteorites** crash into it. These are space rocks that hit a moon or planet. They leave **craters,** or dents. Callisto has more craters than any other moon.

Amazing Moons

Jupiter has many amazing moons. Imagine that you could travel to one of them. Which moon would you visit? Why?

Flyby. *A spacecraft flies toward Jupiter.*

Wordwise

crater: dent in the surface of a planet or moon

meteorite: rock from space that hits a planet or moon

moon: natural object that circles a planet

Moonlight. *Ganymede is larger and has more craters than Earth's moon.*

Pizza Moon. *Io has more volcanoes than any other moon. The volcanoes make the moon look like a pizza.*

Fire and Ice. *Meteorites have blasted thousands of craters into Callisto's surface.*

Our Solar System

Out-of-This-World Facts

- Mercury and Venus are the only planets in the solar system that don't have moons.

- Jupiter, Saturn, Uranus, and Neptune have rings.

- One of Saturn's moons, Mimas, looks like the Death Star from *Star Wars.*

- Uranus is lying on its side.

- Neptune has a dark spot that may be similar to Jupiter's Great Red Spot.

Jupiter

Mars

Earth

Venus

Mercury

The planets in our solar system are different sizes. Their gravity, or pull, is different too. So on some planets you would weigh less than on Earth. On others, you would weigh more. The chart shows what a 60-pound kid would weigh on each.* The drawing shows the eight planets and Pluto.

Mercury	Mars	Uranus
23 pounds	23 pounds	53 pounds
Venus	Jupiter	Neptune
54 pounds	142 pounds	68 pounds
Earth	Saturn	Pluto
60 pounds	64 pounds	4 pounds

* Source: exploratorium.edu/ronh/weight

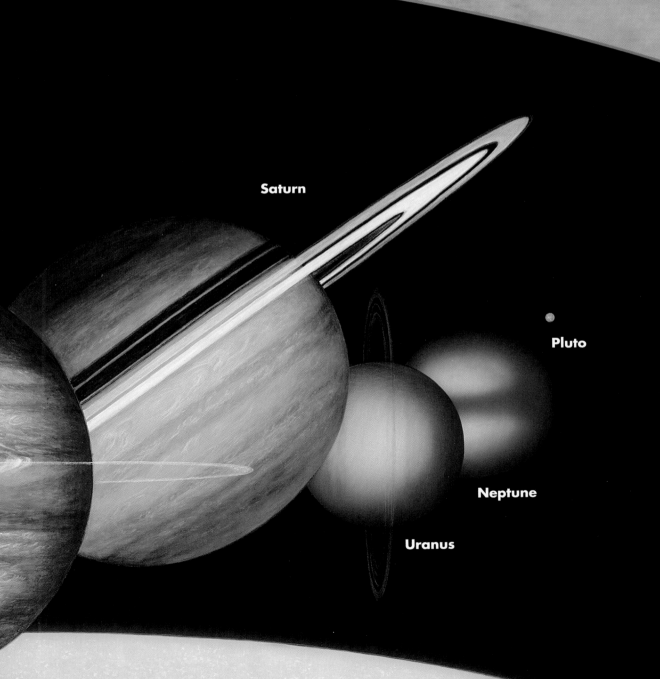

Saturn

Pluto

Neptune

Uranus

NASA

Seeing Into Space

By Ray Villard
Space Telescope Science Institute

Today, we know more about the planets and moons than ever before. Yet each day we learn something new. What is changing our views of space? The Hubble Space Telescope!

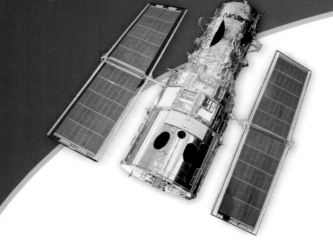

Above It All ▶▶▶▶▶▶▶▶▶▶▶▶

In many ways, Hubble is like any other **telescope.** It is a tool. It makes things that are far away look bigger.

So what makes Hubble special? This telescope travels through space. It circles our planet. Right now, it is 350 miles above Earth. From there, it can see deep into space.

Hubble sends us pictures of what it sees. These help us learn more about our solar system and beyond.

Puzzling Planets ▶▶▶▶▶▶▶

You might think we know everything about space. It is true that we have seen a lot. But we are still learning even more. Our views of space are always changing.

Pluto was once called a planet. Not anymore. You see, no other planet looks like Pluto. It is small. It is even smaller than our moon. It is icy too. And it is far from the sun.

So if Pluto is a not a planet, what is it? Scientists call it a **dwarf planet.** This means it is like a planet, only smaller.

Hubble has found other small, distant worlds. One is called Quar. Another is called Sedna. They are even smaller than Pluto.

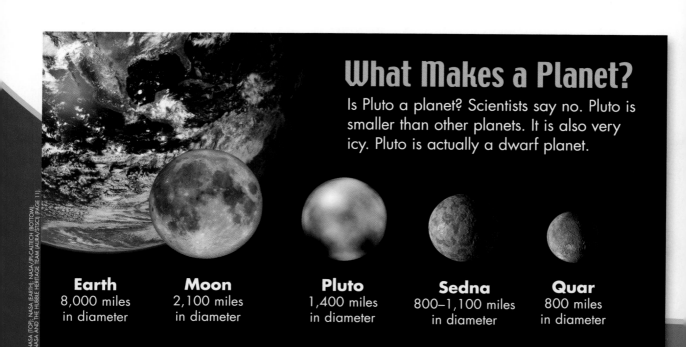

What Makes a Planet?

Is Pluto a planet? Scientists say no. Pluto is smaller than other planets. It is also very icy. Pluto is actually a dwarf planet.

Earth
8,000 miles in diameter

Moon
2,100 miles in diameter

Pluto
1,400 miles in diameter

Sedna
800–1,100 miles in diameter

Quar
800 miles in diameter

Exploding Star.
This cloud of gas lies near the edge of the Milky Way galaxy.

Star Gazing ▶▶▶▶▶▶▶▶▶▶▶

Hubble looks at more than planets. It also shows us many distant stars. Hubble's pictures help us learn how stars form and how they die.

Some of Hubble's most amazing photos show huge clouds of gas. They are called **nebulae.** Some of these clouds are round. They look like fuzzy planets. But they are the remains of old stars.

New Views ▶▶▶▶▶▶▶▶▶▶

Hubble has changed the way we look at space. Soon, a new space telescope will join Hubble. It will also travel high above Earth. We can only imagine the wonders it will show.

Wordwise

dwarf planet: large object smaller than a planet that circles the sun

nebula: cloud of gas in space

telescope: device used to study distant objects

Jupiter

Check out these questions to discover what you have learned about Jupiter.

1 What makes Jupiter an amazing planet?

2 How is Jupiter different from Earth?

3 Describe Jupiter's moons.

4 Why do scientists think Pluto is not a planet?

5 How has the Hubble Space Telescope changed the way we see space?